YOUR LAND AND MY LAND
ASIA

We Visit

INDONESIA

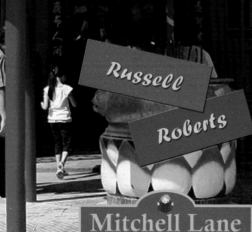

Russell

Roberts

Mitchell Lane

PUBLISHERS
P.O. Box 196
Hockessin, Delaware 19707

YOUR LAND AND MY LAND ASIA

Cambodia
China
India
Indonesia
Japan
Malaysia
North Korea
The Philippines
Singapore
South Korea

YOUR LAND
AND
MY LAND
ASIA

We Visit

INDONESIA

Printing   1   2   3   4   5   6   7   8   9

Library of Congress Cataloging-in-Publication Data
Roberts, Russell, 1953-
  We visit Indonesia / by Russell Roberts.
      pages cm. — (Your land my land: Asia)
  Includes bibliographical references and index.
  Audience: Ages 9-13.
  ISBN 978-1-61228-478-1 (library bound)
  1. Indonesia—History—Juvenile literature. 2. Indonesia—Geography—Juvenile
literature. 3. Indonesia—Social life and customs—Juvenile literature. I. Title.
  DS615.R58 2014
  959.8—dc23
                                                      2013041467
eBook ISBN: 9781612285344

PUBLISHER'S NOTE: This story is based on the author's extensive research,
which he believes to be accurate. Documentation of this research is on
page 61.

      The internet sites referenced herein were active as of the publication date.
Due to the fleeting nature of some websites, we cannot guarantee they will all
be active when you are reading this book.

Contents

Introduction 6
1 A Tsunami Leads to Peace 9
   Where in the World Is Indonesia? 12
   Facts at a Glance 13
2 Indonesia's Early History 15
3 The Rocky Road to Independence 21
4 Famous Indonesians 29
5 An Island Tour 33
6 Indonesia's People and
   Their Customs 39
7 Dining and Drinking 47
8 Celebrations and Commemorations .. 51
Indonesian Recipe:
   Rujak (Spicy Fruit Salad) 56
Indonesian Craft:
   Shadow Puppets and Theater 57
Timeline 58
Chapter Notes 59
Further Reading 60
   Books 60
   On the Internet 60
   Works Consulted 61
Glossary 62
Index 63

Introduction

In Southeast Asia is a remarkable country called Indonesia. It is an archipelago made up of over 17,500 islands, and about 6,000 of these islands are inhabited. Indonesia's population is estimated at about 250 million people, making it the fourth most populous country in the world.

There are over 300 different ethnic groups in Indonesia, speaking more than 700 different languages. Indonesia is the world's largest Muslim nation, and it also contains Christians, Hindus, Buddhists, and other religions. The country's motto is "Unity in Diversity." That means that there is strength in different types of people who come together and act as one.

Indonesia has a long, interesting history. The country contains numerous active volcanoes, and it has an estimated 40,000 plant and 600 animal species. Millions of people go there to enjoy its beautiful beaches and travel through its hot, humid jungles. As you can see, Indonesia certainly has a lot going on!

Would you like to visit this fascinating country? Read on, and discover things you never knew…

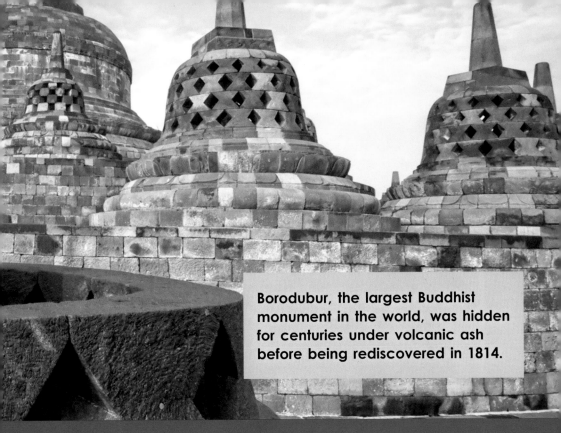

Borodubur, the largest Buddhist monument in the world, was hidden for centuries under volcanic ash before being rediscovered in 1814.

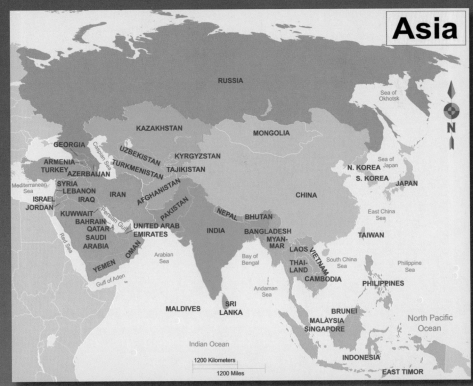

Asia

Trash and debris cover the streets near homes in downtown Banda in Aceh on the Indonesian island of Sumatra following the massive tsunami on December 26, 2004.

A Tsunami
Leads to Peace

December 26, 2004, dawned just like any typical day in Indonesia. The sun shone down brightly. Everything seemed normal.

What no one could know was that it would be a very different day for Indonesia—a day that would bring great tragedy. However, out of this terrible tragedy would ultimately come something good.

When a natural disaster strikes Indonesia, it is often related to volcanoes or volcanic eruptions. The country has over 100 active volcanoes. These volcanoes can erupt at any time, causing destruction and death. One of the most well-known volcanic eruptions in history happened in Indonesia in 1883. It was a volcano called Krakatau. Because of this, people associate volcanoes with Indonesia. They do not usually think of tsunamis.

Yet a tsunami was exactly what was about to happen to Indonesia... and more precisely, to a region at the northern end of the island of Sumatra called Aceh. Populated by more than four million people, Aceh is thought to be where the religion of Islam began to spread throughout Indonesia.

For more than 25 years, Aceh had been at war with the government of Indonesia. The people in Aceh practice a stricter version of Islam than the rest of the country. Those

FYI FACT:

In 2006, tsunami waves from an earthquake surged more than 600 feet (183 meters) inland on Java.

religious differences were one reason that the war had begun. Aceh wanted to be independent from Indonesia. Now Fate was about to take over.

A few minutes before 8:00 AM, a mammoth earthquake occurred on the floor of the Indian Ocean off the west coast of Sumatra. The earthquake measured 9.0 on the Richter Scale, which measures the intensity and power of earthquakes. According to the Centre for Remote Imaging, Sensing and Processing (CRISP) at the National University of Singapore, it

The Krakatau volcanic eruption in 1883 was heard 3,000 miles (4,800 kilometers) away, making it what some people consider the loudest sound in modern history.

was the fourth-largest earthquake in the world since 1900.[1]

The incredible amount of force that was unleashed caused super shock waves, which moved an enormous amount of seawater. This caused the gigantic waves known as tsunamis to form and begin racing across the ocean toward Aceh.

Since tsunamis are rare in the Indian Ocean, there were no early warning systems to alert people when one was approaching. It slammed into the Aceh coastline like a freight train plowing into a house of cards. People ran in all directions as the giant wall of water smashed onto the land and surged forward at frightening speed. The water crushed and destroyed homes and buildings. Trees snapped like tiny twigs in a hurricane wind. Animals ran to higher ground.

While other countries were affected by the tsunami, Indonesia—especially Aceh—was hit the hardest. The raging water killed more

FYI FACT:

India is building a tsunami early warning system for the South China Sea that will serve Indonesia.

than 130,000 Indonesians and another 37,000 were missing. Approximately 500,000 people became homeless. Some coastal villages lost nearly 70 percent of their population. Fishing and agriculture in Aceh were greatly damaged and it is estimated that nearly 50% of the people in the province lost their way of earning a living.[2]

Yet at this tragic moment, Indonesians showed why they are part of such a remarkable country. The Aceh conflict had killed an estimated 15,000 people and disrupted the lives of thousands more. It seemed like it would go on and on.

When the tsunami struck, both the government and the Free Aceh Movement realized they needed to stop fighting to help the region recover from this devastating tragedy. The two sides, which had not been able to find common ground for decades, rolled up their sleeves and went to work to resolve their differences. Within a year, they reached a peace agreement.

It was a classic example of unity in diversity. The Indonesian people, separated by differences in belief, had come together in a time of tragedy.

Weeks after the December 26 tsunami, injured people were still being found by rescue workers.

Where in the World

Indonesia

International boundary
★ National capital
Railroad
Road

0   200   400 Kilometers
0   200   400
Mercator Projection

INDONESIA FACTS AT A GLANCE

Official Country Name: Republic of Indonesia

Official Language: Bahasa Indonesia (official), English, Dutch, local dialects

Population: 251,160,124 (July 2013 estimate)

Total Area: 735,358 square miles (1,904,569 square kilometers); slightly less than three times the size of Texas

Land Area: 699,451 square miles (1,811,569 square kilometers)

Water Area: 35,908 square miles (93,000 square kilometers)

Capital: Jakarta

Government: Republic

Ethnic Makeup: Javanese 40.6%, Sundanese 15%, several specific groups less than 4% each, other or unspecified 29.9%

Religions: Muslim 86.1%, Protestant 5.7%, Roman Catholic 3%, Hindu 1.8%, other 3.4%

Agricultural products: rubber and similar products, palm oil, poultry, beef, forest products, shrimp, cocoa, coffee, medicinal herbs, essential oils, fish and similar products, spices

Industries: : petroleum and natural gas, textiles, automotive, electrical appliances, apparel, footwear, mining, cement, medical instruments and appliances, handicrafts, chemical fertilizers, plywood, rubber, processed food, jewelry, tourism

Climate: Tropical—hot and humid; more moderate in highlands

Lowest point: Indian Ocean

Highest Point: Puncak Jaya in Papua Province on the island of New Guinea—16,024 feet (4,844 meters)

Flag: two equal horizontal bands of red (on top, symbolizing courage) and white (representing purity); the colors derive from the banner of the Majapahit Empire of the 13th–15th centuries

National Symbol: Garuda Pancasila (mythical bird)

National anthem: "Indonesia Raya" ("Great Indonesia")

Source: CIA World Factbook -
https://www.cia.gov/library/publications/the-world-factbook/geos/id.html

In early days, growing rice in paddies such as these helped to establish permanent villages that would one day become part of the country of Indonesia.

Indonesia's Early History

About 4000 BCE (Before the Common Era), people from southern China and Indochina called the Malays came to the area that is now Indonesia. They brought with them a culture of rice-growing techniques that featured irrigation. By about 700 BCE, Indonesia contained many permanent villages centered around rice production.

Around the first century CE (Common Era), many of these small villages grouped themselves together as kingdoms. They began making contact with other groups of traders from Southeast Asia.

One of the first prominent trading empires from Indonesia was called Sriwijaya. It flourished on the coast of Sumatra over a thousand years ago. Merchants from Persia, India, and Arabia brought their goods to Sriwijaya and traded them for local goods and products from other countries, such as China. Indonesia was known for its spices, gold, and benzoin, a gum-like substance valued by the Chinese.

As trading flourished among the various groups, their cultures intermixed. It is believed that this is how Hinduism and Buddhism came to Indonesia—from contact with those cultures from India.

Early in the eighth century, another great kingdom called Mataram developed in Java. Unlike Sriwijaya, which was a trading empire, Mataram was an agricultural society. Mataram eventually became part of the Buddhist kingdom of Sailendra. Sailendra built a magnificent temple complex called Borobudur. It is the largest Buddhist monument in the world.

The last great Hindu kingdom in Indonesia, called Majapahit, emerged in the thirteenth century. Under its most famous ruler, King Hayam Wuruk, and Prime Minister Gajah Mada, the era of the Majapahit kingdom is often called a "golden age" of Indonesia.[1] Not only did Majapahit control and influence much of Indonesia, it also maintained relations with other countries such as China, Cambodia, Annam (today part of Vietnam), and Siam (today called Thailand). The Majapahit kingdom remained strong until Wuruk died in 1389.

The first area in which Islam took hold was northern Sumatra, possibly because of the Arab traders who had settled there. In 1292, when Marco Polo visited Aceh, he reported that the people there had converted to Islam. Islam spread across the trade routes, and was soon established across Indonesia.

Although Marco Polo and a few other Europeans had previously visited Indonesia, the first to come to the country in large numbers were the Portuguese. They were after the rich Asian trade routes and control of the spice trade. Not only were the spices desirable for their great flavor, they were also thought to have medicinal value. Spices such as cloves, nutmeg, and mace were considered cures for everything from the plague to venereal disease.[2]

Other European countries such as Spain, England, and the Netherlands soon came to Indonesia to challenge the Portuguese. The Dutch government formed the Vereenigde Oost-Indische Compagnie (VOC), the Dutch East India Company. The VOC had the power to wage war and make treaties as well as conduct trade. Eventually the VOC became the controlling interest in Indonesia. By way of an agreement with the King of Mataram in Java, only VOC ships (or those with VOC permission) were allowed to participate in the spice trade. Using its power and influence, the VOC dictated the winners of wars on Java between local tribes competing for power. Thus the VOC moved from its roots as a trading company to the administration of a colonial empire.

However, the VOC was in decline by the middle of the 18th century, weakened financially and militarily. The VOC turned to the

Marco Polo was a merchant from Venice, Italy, who traveled extensively in Asia and wrote a famous book about his experiences entitled *The Travels of Marco Polo*.

Dutch government for financial help, but an investigation revealed mismanagement and corruption. In 1799 the Dutch government ended the VOC and took control of the company's holdings in Indonesia.

For more than 100 years the Dutch ruled Indonesia. The natives fought against colonial rule. Wars in Java, Borneo, Bali, Aceh, and Sumatra protested rule by the Dutch and their colonial policies, which were often harsh and repressive.

This engraving by 19th century French sailor and explorer Louis Isidore Duperrey shows an Indonesian village on the island of Buru.

Independence from Dutch rule remained a constant desire in Indonesia. On May 20, 1908, a doctor in Java named Wahidin Soedirohoesodo and his students formed a political group called the Budi Utomo, or "Beautiful Endeavor." It was one of the first associations dedicated to the goal of Indonesian independence. Today May 20 is celebrated as National Awakening Day and is a public holiday. Four years later, a group of Islamic traders formed the Sarekat Islam (SI) as a movement to counter Chinese influence in the batik trade. The group soon broadened its appeal and became more of an anti-colonial organization.

Another leading nationalist movement got its start as a splinter group within the SI in 1920. This was the Partai Komunis Indonesia (PKI)—the Indonesia Communist Party. In 1926 the group initiated uprisings in Java and West Sumatra. The Dutch jailed PKI leaders and exiled many members.

However, once the independence door was pried open it was impossible to slam it closed. In 1927 Sukarno (many Javanese have only a single name) founded the Partai Nasional Indonesia (PNI). The PNI was the first secular (non-religious) political party in Indonesia whose goal was independence. Sukarno was arrested and PNI members harassed by the Dutch. The following year the All Indonesian Youth Congress proclaimed the ideals of one national identity, one country, and one language.

When World War II erupted in 1939, and Germany occupied the Netherlands the following year, many people thought Dutch colonial rule would end. But the Dutch government in exile held onto Indonesia, and not much changed.

Little did Indonesians realize the momentous events that were about to occur.

Sukarno demands independence from Dutch rule as he addresses a rally of more than 200,000 people in the city of Macassar, the largest city on Sulawesi. He became the first president of Indonesia.

Chapter 3

The Rocky Road to Independence

On March 5, 1942, the Japanese Army occupied Batavia, Indonesia's capital city. The Dutch colonial government promptly surrendered. Suddenly Indonesia was finally free from Dutch rule.

Initially the Indonesians greeted the Japanese as liberators. Japan allowed Sukarno and other nationalist leaders to return from exile and gave Indonesians low-level government positions that had previously been closed to them. They even changed the name of Batavia back to its former name of Jakarta.

However, the Indonesians soon realized that they had merely swapped the Dutch for the Japanese as their rulers. The Japanese made Indonesians work on projects designed to help Japan in its wartime efforts. They also organized Indonesians into an army they hoped would fight an anticipated Allied invasion.

The Japanese surrender in August, 1945, set off a confused situation in Indonesia. The victorious Allies sent no troops immediately to Indonesia to form a temporary government, so the Japanese remained in charge. Concerned that the Dutch might come back to fill the vacuum, Sukarno was pressured to declare the country independent. He did so on August 17, 1945, reading a proclamation from his Jakarta home. That date is still celebrated in the country as Indonesia's independence day. Sukarno became its first president the following day.

However, when the British landed troops in Jakarta in October, 1945, Dutch troops came with them. It quickly became apparent that the Netherlands intended to regain control of Indonesia and ignore

The Japanese Navy played a key role in the invasion of Indonesia in World War II. It almost completely annihilated opposing warships during a series of battles early in 1942 while suffering minimal losses.

any attempts at independence. The British soon pulled out of Indonesia, and for the next several years the Dutch fought the Indonesian nationalistic forces. However, world opinion was turning against the Dutch. Pressured by the United States and the United Nations, the Netherlands negotiated for Indonesia's independence. On December 27, 1949, the Dutch finally acknowledged Indonesia's independence.

Independence did not immediately solve Indonesia's problems. In the following years, rebel groups such as the Darul Islam (Islamic Domain) battled the government. The country's economy struggled to recover from its poor handling by the Japanese during World War II. Sukarno continued to consolidate power for himself while aligning Indonesia with communist elements and against the United States and other Western countries.

Then, in September 1965, General Suharto seized power and began reversing much of what Sukarno had done. He improved relations with the West and tried to strengthen the economy. In March, 1967 he became president.

In reality, however, Indonesia had exchanged one dictator for another. Suharto became the absolute ruler. He brutally dealt with dissension from rebel groups seeking a different or separate government. In 1976 Indonesia seized the eastern part of the island of Timor, which had once been a Portuguese colony. The remainder of Timor had been a Dutch possession. A resistance movement to Indonesian rule immediately began, fueled in part by the fact that East Timor was

Indonesian President Suharto delivers his state of the nation address on August 16, 1995. That was one day before the 50th anniversary of the country's declaration of independence.

mainly populated by Catholics and Indonesia was primarily a Muslim country. The conflict dragged on for years, killing thousands, with neither side able to defeat the other.

In 1997 a financial crisis that greatly affected Indonesia swept through Asia. Foreign debt rose, inflation ravaged the country, and millions lost their jobs as the economy struggled. Banks collapsed, and fearful Indonesians were faced with losing their life savings.

In the midst of all this financial turmoil, Suharto was re-elected in February, 1998. It had been a foregone conclusion that he would win again since he still controlled the country, but Indonesians upset by conditions began demonstrating against him.

In early May, 1998 Jakarta erupted in violence and rioting. An estimated 1,200 people died, and over 6,000 buildings were damaged or destroyed.[1] Anti-Suharto demonstrations continued after the riots were over, and it was obvious that the aging president had lost the confidence of his people. On May 21, 1998 he resigned, ending more than 32 years in power. He was replaced by Vice President B.J. Habibie.

In early 1999, with East Timor still seething with unrest, Habibie announced that he would let the country vote to remain with Indonesia or seek its independence. However, Indonesian-backed militia tried to intimidate the population into voting for Indonesia through killings and other acts of violence. Nevertheless, nearly 80 percent of East Timorans voted to secede from Indonesia. East Timor became independent in 2002.

Still Indonesia did not find peace. A nightclub in Bali was bombed by terrorists in October, 2002, killing more than 200 people. The

FYI FACT:

When Suharto became Indonesia's president, his economic policy was known as the New Order.

Election officials count ballots from the presidential elections in East Timor in April 2002. Xanana Gusmão was declared the winner. East Timor officially gained its independence the following month.

FYI FACT:

United States President Barack Obama visited Indonesia in 2010 and praised its diversity and democracy. As a child he lived in the country for four years, from 1967 to 1971.

Marriott Hotel in Jakarta was attacked in August 2003, killing 12 people and injuring 150. Bali suffered further attacks in 2005.

It even seemed as if Nature had decided to cause problems for Indonesia. After the devastating tsunami of December, 2004, the country was struck by several more earthquakes and tsunamis. On May 26, 2006, Java was hit by an earthquake and subsequent tsunami that killed more than 6,000 people. Less than two months later another earthquake hit Java, killing another 500 people. In February, 2007, floods surged through Jakarta, leaving nearly 350,000 people homeless.

Indonesia needed all the unity through diversity it could find to deal with all these crisis situations. However, the country kept moving forward, seeking to become a model democratic country in Southeast Asia. In recent years Indonesia has made great strides toward democracy, particularly with their last two presidential elections. In 2004 Susilo Bambang Yudhoyono was elected president of Indonesia. In 2009 he was re-elected, becoming the first person to be re-elected.

Indonesia today is a federal republic, with a president elected for a five-year term. The People's Consultative Assembly (Majelis Permusyawaratan Rakyat, or MPR) is the upper house of the Indonesian Parliament. It consists of members of the DPR and DPD (see below) and plays a role in inaugurating and impeaching the president and in amending the constitution. However, it does not create national policy.

The Indonesian House of Representatives is the Dewan Perwakilan Rakyat (DPR). It contains 560 seats. Its members are elected to five-year terms. The DPR creates and passes legislation at the national level. The House of Regional Representatives (Dewan Perwakilan Daerah, or DPD) provides legislative input to the DPR on issues affecting regions. It contains 132 members, four from each of Indonesia's original 30 provinces, two special regions, and a special capital city district.

Suharto meets with his cabinet soon after assuming the presidency in 1967. He promised to improve the Indonesian economy, yet was forced out three decades later due to an economic crisis.

Famous Indonesians

Hayam Wuruk (1334–1389) was the king of Majapahit during the height of its power and influence in the 14th century. His mother was Queen Tribhuwana, the daughter of the founder of Majapahit. At the age of 16, in 1350, Hayam Wuruk became king. According to contemporary accounts, he was handsome, intelligent, talented, and excelled in archery, fencing, art, music and dancing. Guided by his prime minister, Ganja Mada, he extended Majapahit's power throughout Indonesia and even beyond. Unfortunately, he didn't have an heir through his official queen. So when he died, he had arranged to divide the kingdom between a nephew and a son by a lesser queen. Conflict between the two men resulted in civil war and fatally weakened the Majapahit kingdom.

Suharto (1921–2008) kept Indonesia in his iron grip for more than 30 years. He was born in the Javanese village of Kemusuk, and his parents divorced when he was still an infant. He lived much of his early life with foster parents. His military career began in the Indonesian security forces assembled by the Japanese during their World War II occupation of Indonesia. Joining the Indonesian Army after the war, he became a major general when Indonesia achieved independence.

In early October, 1965, Suharto and his forces defeated a coup attempt against Indonesian president Sukarno. Within two years Suharto had replaced Sukarno as Indonesia's president. Suharto began what he called a "New Order" for Indonesia. He was strictly anti-communist, which won him the support of western countries. Under his leadership, Indonesia enjoyed economic growth and improved standards of living. However, he stumbled badly by invading East Timor in 1975, leading to a war he could not win and eventually resulting in more than 100,000 deaths. His government was also extremely corrupt.

In 1998 Suharto was forced to resign, following widespread demonstrations and an economic crisis. He died on January 27, 2008.

Sukarno (1901–1970) was the first president of an independent Indonesia. He was born in Surabaya, in eastern Java. He was first named Kusno Sosrodihardjo, which his parents later changed to Sukarno. In 1927 he and others formed the Partai Nasional Indonesia (PNI), which began agitating for Indonesia's independence from the Dutch. When the Japanese took control of Indonesia in World War II, Sukarno cooperated with them in the hopes that they would keep the Dutch away.

When the Japanese surrendered in August, 1945, Sukarno declared Indonesia independent. As Indonesia's first president, Sukarno had limited power. However, he felt that western-style democracy would never work well in Indonesia, and kept grabbing more and more power for himself until he ruled as dictator. Finally he was ousted as president in a coup led by Suharto on March 12, 1967 and placed under house arrest. He died three years later.

Raden Adjeng Kartini (1879–1904) is recognized as Indonesia's first feminist. She was born into a noble family in Mayong, Java. When she reached adolescence, tradition dictated that she leave her schooling for a life of isolation to prepare her for marriage. She wrote bitterly about being unable to pursue her education and about other

Sukarno's daughter Megawati Sukarnoputri served as Indonesia's first female president from 2001 to 2004.

gender equality issues, such as the custom of forced marriages for Indonesian women.

Her own marriage, arranged by her father, destroyed her chances of accepting an offer to study abroad. With her husband's approval and assistance from the Dutch government, she opened the first Indonesian primary school for native girls that did not discriminate on the basis of their social status. The school taught a progressive, Western-style curriculum.

On September 17, 1904, Kartini died of complications from giving birth to her first child. Seven years later, a book of her letters entitled *From Darkness to Light: Thoughts About and on Behalf of the Javanese People* was published and became an international sensation. To this day in Indonesia, Kartini Day is still celebrated on her birthday.

Affandi (1907–1990) is considered one of the greatest painters in Indonesia's history. Born in West Java as the son of a surveyor, Affandi became a self-taught artist. Early on he worked at numerous odd jobs. One was painting houses. He would save leftover paint for himself.

In the 1940s, after the Japanese surrender, Affandi became involved in making posters supporting Indonesia's independence. As time went on he became a recognized master of the expressionistic style. He never used either a palette or brushes. Rather, he would smear paint on his thumb and transfer it directly to a canvas. He could spend weeks studying a subject but the actual painting would take no more than 90 minutes. The process would end when he felt his emotion for the work fading.

Affandi died in 1990. His home, with a unique, banana-shaped roof, is now a museum.

Mount Semeru is the highest mountain on Java and one of the most active volcanoes in Indonesia. Its most recent eruption was in 2012.

An Island Tour

Indonesia is the world's largest island nation. The inhabited islands of Indonesia are classified into three groups. The large islands—Sumatra, Java, Kalimantan (also called Borneo), and Sulawesi—are known as the Greater Sundas. This is where a majority of the Indonesian population lives. The chain of smaller islands east of Java (from Bali to Lombok, Sumbawa, Sumba, and Flores to Timor) composes the Lesser Sundas. The third area is located east of Sulawesi and north of the Lesser Sundas. It is called the Moluccas.

Java is considered the focal point of Indonesia. Over 115 million people live in Java, which is around the size of the state of New York.[1] Java accounts for just seven percent of Indonesia's total land mass, yet contains over 60 percent of its population.[2]

Java is dominated by volcanoes. They form a line that runs from one end of the island to the other. This is one of the most active portions of the Ring of Fire, which extends in a rough horseshoe shape from New Zealand through Indonesia and Japan to the Aleutian Islands. From there it skirts the west coasts of North, Central and South America—a total distance of about 25,000 miles (40,000 kilometers). Ironically, these Javanese volcanoes are responsible for the island's rich and fertile soil. Eruptions deposit lava and ash onto the ground, and this material is high in nutrients that encourage plant growth.

Java has over 20 volcanoes that have been active since 1600. The highest is Mt. Semeru, which rises 12,060 feet (3,676 meters). The island is just a few miles from one of the most famous volcanoes in the world—Krakatau. More than 35,000 people are thought to have been killed when it erupted on August 26, 1883, although the death toll may have been much higher. The ash in the atmosphere lingered for two years. The eruption caused four different tsunamis, each with wave heights of more than 100 feet (30 meters). The tsunamis killed everyone on the island of Sebesi, the island closest to the volcano.

Amazingly, even though Java is so heavily populated, 63 percent of the land is cultivated, compared to just 10-20 percent on other Indonesian islands.[3] About 55 percent of the population consists of farmers, and the crop of greatest importance is rice. Other crops include maize, soybeans, peanuts, cassavas, and potatoes.

Sumatra is the fourth largest island in the world, after Greenland, New Guinea, and Kalimantan. It is about the size of California. It has a population of 40 million people, more than 20 percent of Indonesia's total population.[4] Like most of the rest of Indonesia, it has a hot, humid climate. Sumatra used to be covered by tropical rain forests, but in recent years has lost a good portion due to development.

Sumatra contains a large variety of wildlife. It has almost 200 different species of mammals, some of which are found nowhere else in the world. Among these are the Sumatran rabbit, the Sumatran weasel, and several different types of squirrels and bats. It also contains elephants, big cats such as tigers, apes, rhinoceroses, pigs, tapirs, bears, orangutans, and numerous types of birds and fish. Some of its species are critically endangered, such as the Sumatran tiger and orangutan.

The island also contains the largest flower in the world—the rafflesia. This unusual plant has no leaves, stems, or roots. It is a parasitic plant that grows on the stem and roots of a climbing vine. When its flower buds open, it has a very foul smell, much like rotting meat. It is known locally as the "corpse flower."[5]

FYI FACT:

The lesser mouse deer of Indonesia is only one foot (30 centimeters) tall.

Sumatra has a vast amount of natural resources. Coal, tin, bauxite, oil, gold, natural gas, timber,

Jakarta, Indonesia's capital and largest city, is one of the fastest-growing cities in the world. Its total urban area is the second-largest in the world, while the city itself ranks 13th with a population exceeding 10,000,000.

rubber, tea, palm oil, cacao, and coffee account for more than half of the export income of Indonesia.

Lying hundreds of miles to the east of Sumatra and Java, Sulawesi has four "arms" stretching out from its "body" and looks like a misshapen spider. It has also been compared to a giant crab, an orchid, and even a bizarrely-shaped starfish. However, even though it covers an area nearly as large as Great Britain, no place is further than 25 miles (40 kilometers) from the sea. It was in Sulawesi that Victorian-age naturalist Alfred Russel Wallace wrote down his ideas on evolution. He sent letters describing these ideas to Charles Darwin, prompting Darwin to write his classic work *Origin of Species*.[6]

Indonesia's precious rain forests, such as this one on Sumatra, are being destroyed by widespread logging.

Sulawesi is mountainous, with nearly a dozen active volcanoes and numerous lakes. It has a population of over 17 million people, many of whom make their living from the sea because the mountains prevent agriculture. Sulawesi also exports numerous minerals, such as nickel, gold, sulfur, and iron ore.

Conservation is very important on Sulawesi because of the large number of endemic mammal species. These include the ferocious dwarf buffalo, which is about the size of a large dog. Forest destruction is a major problem here.

The final Greater Sunda Island is Borneo, the world's third-largest island. It is divided among Indonesia, Malaysia, and the sultanate of Brunei. The Indonesian section is called Kalimantan, and occupies about two-thirds of the island. Brunei is very small (2,226 square miles, or 5,765 square kilometers), with the Malaysian states of Sarawak and Sabah occupying the rest.

The entire island is an exotic region of dense jungles, wild animals, and headhunters. Unfortunately, destruction of forests and excess logging have destroyed much of the island's once-mysterious jungles.

While there are numerous tribes living on Kalimantan that use their own separate names, they are referred to collectively as the Dayaks. The Dayaks used to practice headhunting, but fortunately it has largely died out. Indeed, many aspects of the Dayaks' traditional way of life, such as living in large communal buildings called longhouses and women stretching their ear lobes with heavy gold or brass rings, have disappeared as development and modern society keep encroaching upon them.

About 11 million people live in Kalimantan. Often the island's many rivers and other waterways are used to move people and products, much like highways in other countries. Tourism is not a big feature

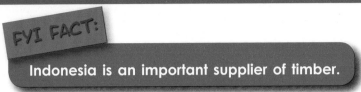

of Kalimantan, but many of those who choose to visit go to see the orangutans.

Among the other Indonesian islands, Bali is the best-known. About four million people live on Bali, including most of Indonesia's minority Hindu population. It is Indonesia's most popular vacation spot, drawing tourists from all over the world. Terrorist bombings in 2002 and 2005 temporarily slowed the flow of visitors, but tourism has regained its balance in the last few years. Bali offers a variety of attractions for visitors: shopping, dining, exploring, sightseeing, or just relaxing on its famous beaches.

Lakes and rivers play an important part in Indonesia. Many lakes are inside what once were volcanoes. Some of these lakes flood in the rainy season and then dry up so completely in the dry season that people can travel across them.

One of the most spectacular lakes in all of Indonesia is gigantic Lake Toba on Sumatra. If it were in the state of New York, it would reach from the Statue of Liberty to West Point—a distance that would take over an hour to drive. Lake Toba is the world's largest and deepest volcanic lake. It is the result of a massive volcanic explosion that occurred many years ago. The explosion killed many people and caused the temperature of the planet to drop by several degrees because of all the material it shot into the atmosphere, which partially blocked the warming rays of the sun. The explosion also created a large island called Samosir, which is nearly the size of Singapore (275 square miles, or 710 square kilometers) in the middle of the lake.

The rafflesia flower only lasts for a few days, so it is very difficult to locate when in bloom. The destruction of the rain forests is also destroying its natural habitat.

A Javanese wayang kulit performance of the legend of the five Pandava brothers. According to the story, the brothers were all married to the same woman (Draupadi), and fought a great war with their cousins.

Chapter 6

Indonesia's People and Their Customs

With all the various groups of people who have come into contact with Indonesia throughout the centuries of trading, it's not surprising that there are so many ethnic groups in the country. While transportation, education, the influence of multiple societies, and other factors are blurring the distinctions among ethnic groups, some distinct cultural identification remains. Let's briefly look at some of the most notable groups in Indonesia.

SUMATRA

Acenese—Primarily residents of northern Sumatra. They often engage in agriculture, but are recognized as skillful metal workers, weavers, potters, and boat builders.

Batak—They reside in the interior of north/central Sumatra around Lake Toba. Anthropologists consider them as representatives of the ancient Malay culture that once existed in Indonesia. Their houses have roofs with large gable ends and carved buffalo horns.

Minangkabau—Like the Batak, they have unique houses, with large sweeping roofs. Women are held in high esteem by the Minangkabu. They run the household and pass down inheritances through their side of the family, rather than through the male side. They mainly live in west-central Sumatra.

JAVA

Javanese—The most common ethnic group in Indonesia. The Javanese often only have one name, but those in the upper class will choose a family name. These family names reflect status, such as elder or younger, rather than male or female. The Javanese are famous for the wayang kulit (shadow play), which uses leather puppets. Wayang kulit performances on Java feature musical accompaniment by bronze gongs and other percussive instruments.

Sundanese—The Sundanese culture is similar to that of the Javanese but contains slight differences. For example, rather than leather puppets in their version of the wayang kulit, they employ wooden puppets and flute music rather than percussion.

Badui—The Badui live in western Java in relative isolation. They believe that writing has magical power. The inner Badui villages avoid contact with the outside world. The outer villages don't particularly try to avoid outside contact, but exhibit little interest in the modern world.

BALI

Balinese—The Balinese and their culture are extremely well-known both in and out of Bali. They have developed elaborate performances of ritual storytelling for visitors. Rice is a primary crop, and is grown in fields with extensive irrigation systems.

SULAWESI

Toraja—Known for their distinctive houses on stilts with roofs upturned on both ends, the Toraja are primarily agricultural workers. They practice cliff burial, in which likenesses of the dead are placed in open areas of cliffs.

Bugis—The Bugis are related to the Toraja. They are well-known seafarers, who still trade between the islands in ships with colorful sails. The Bugis also manufacture silk that is among the best in the region.

The Toraja people on the island of Sulawesi have very distinctive-looking traditional houses.

Minahasa—Most of the Minahasa practice agriculture, which is accompanied by festivals, feasting, and ceremony at the times of planting and harvesting. They live primarily in northern Sulawesi.

KALIMANTAN
Dayak—Despite their fierce reputation, the Dayak people are friendly to outsiders. They gather produce from the jungle, farm, fish, and hunt. Sometimes they still hunt the way their ancestors did, with spear and blowpipe.

THE CHINESE

Among the many foreign nationalities with a presence in Indonesia, the Chinese are the most significant. It is estimated that the Chinese comprise three percent of the country's population. Most Chinese live in Java, eastern Sumatra, and western Kalimantan.

The Chinese arrived in Indonesia in significant numbers in the 19th century. They were recruited by the Dutch colonial government as laborers for mines and agriculture. According to the law at that time, the Chinese were not allowed to own land. They became merchants, bankers, and businessmen instead. Over time they became an important part of the Indonesian economy. Today there are many Chinese in positions of financial power in Indonesia. However, it has not been easy for the Chinese in Indonesia. They have had to endure prejudice, anger, and violence.

Despite all these differences, one thing remains central in Indonesia: the family. For Indonesians, their status, security, and position in society depend on the family. The head of the family is usually the eldest male, known as the bapak. Family members are ranked according to age, not sex. The parents occupy the position of highest honor, but in families with a lot of children, an older relative can act as an "aunt" or "uncle." Some older children in a large family may even live with other relatives for a time.

In the United States, the size of a house indicates wealth or value. While that is sometimes true in Indonesia, more often the size of a house signifies the size of the family living within it. The bigger the house, the bigger the family. Traditional Indonesian houses reflect the country's tropical climate. They are built in an open style, to allow air to circulate. The windows usually have shutters, which serve two purposes: kept open to allow air and light to enter, or kept closed to keep out direct sunlight or wind-driven rain. Once electricity became widely available, many homes got ceiling fans to help move the air. Porches and verandas are common features of Indonesian homes so that people can sit outside.

Building a house on stilts is another way to encourage air circulation, and traditional Indonesian homes often had this feature. Having the house raised on stilts also protected it against flooding. The area below the home could provide storage if needed.

Many family members may live in the same house. The concept of personal or private property is not often practiced. Instead, wealth is shared among family members as needed.

Indonesian parents and their children are very close, and maintain relationships with each other even after the children marry and begin their own families.

FYI FACT:

Many Indonesians bathe twice a day.

In contrast to Western society, children are expected to care for their parents for their entire life, rather than moving away and leaving the parents to fend for themselves. If children do live somewhere else, they still are expected to contribute to their parents' needs. Older kids also look after their younger brothers and sisters.

Children are greatly appreciated in Indonesia. The traditional method of carrying young children in a shoulder sling called a sledang increases the strength of the relationship between mother and child.

This same respect for age and ranking exists for Indonesians when they meet visitors. They will politely try to find out as much as they can about a guest's personal life, such as marital status, if they have any children, and so forth. Such personal questions may seem odd, but to an Indonesian they are necessary. Such questions help them establish the proper way they should address and treat a person they have just met. Indeed, not asking such questions would be rude and discourteous. By the same token, foreign visitors are also expected to ask such questions, as a matter of showing proper respect to Indonesians.

Although Bahasa Indonesia is the official language of the country and is an easy language to learn and speak, different words may mean the same thing. For instance, no one word means "hello." Instead, the correct Indonesian greeting depends upon the time of day: "Selamat pagi" ("Good morning"), "Selamat siang" ("Good afternoon"), "Selamat sore" ("Good evening"), and "Selamat malam" ("Good night").

Harmony, meaning spiritual peace and tranquility, is very important to Indonesians. This means that people—residents and visitors alike—are expected to act in a manner that produces harmony. Creating a scene in public or private—getting angry, shouting, causing embarrassment, and so forth—is greatly disliked by Indonesians. Saving face is very important.

FYI FACT:

Automobiles are sometimes not practical in traffic-choked sections of Indonesia, so people may use other methods of transportation such as these three-wheeled becaks.

Indonesians dislike saying "no." They have numerous ways to indicate a negative. The phrase "tidak usah" means "not necessary," while "tidak boleh" means "not allowed to," and "tidak senang" means "not happy." While this may seem quite unnecessary for those who like to get right to the point, it is based upon the Indonesian notion of saving face. To reject something outright does not save face, while using a gentler phrase will usually keep the door open for a compromise in which everyone saves face.

By the same token, it is important for a visitor to keep face. Acting angry or causing public embarrassment will cause that person to lose face with Indonesians and lower the respect in which he or she is held.

Indonesians enjoy a wide variety of foods, with natural items like fruits and vegetables playing a major role in their diet.

Dining and Drinking

Rice is the main ingredient in the Indonesian diet, and people consume it at all three meals in a day. Some may enjoy noodles and bread rather than rice, but for a majority of people rice is their staple dish.

Fruit is another favorite food among Indonesians. Some varieties are familiar to Western cultures, such as watermelons, guavas, and mangos. Others are virtually unknown, such as rambutan and durian. Rambutan comes from the Malay word "hairy," and refers to the hair-like covering of the fruit. Once the covering is peeled away, the fruit can be eaten. It has a grapelike sweet and sour flavor. The durian is a large fruit whose spiky appearance looks like it belongs in a horror movie as some type of weapon, not on the dinner table. The durian also has a powerful aroma that people either find pleasing or terrible. Some hotels and restaurants have banned the durian because of its strong odor. However, the flesh of this fruit is considered very tasty and is certainly an Indonesian delicacy. You just have to get past the smell!

Indonesians like their food hot, as in spicy. However, Indonesian food is at a level of hot/spicy that usually surprises foreign guests. Even people who think they can handle spicy food are likely to look for the water glass when they order food prepared the typical Indonesian way.

Since Indonesia is so large and diverse, and contains so many different cultures, different people/cultures in different areas have their own special likes and dislikes. For instance, the Sundanese in West

Java enjoy fresh vegetables. People joke that the vegetables do not even have to be picked, but left in the garden and the Sundanese will be happy. In addition, they like tea without sugar. Other Javanese, however, prefer their food to be sweet.

When eating, portions are usually cut small. It is considered good form to take small extra portions rather than piling food onto a plate. Many Indonesians will leave a little bit of food on their plate to indicate when they have had enough to eat.

Food is often eaten by hand, because many Indonesians believe that it tastes better when eaten that way rather than with utensils. According to the belief system of Islam, the left hand is considered unclean. Therefore food can only eaten using the right hand. When utensils are used it usually means only a spoon and fork. Food is cut up into such small pieces that a knife isn't necessary.

Padang restaurants are extremely common in Indonesia. These establishments offer a style of eating that came originally from Padang in Sumatra. Padang restaurants do not have a menu. Rather, plates of plain rice, spicy meat, fish, and vegetables are offered. The diner pays only for that which he/she eats.

Another common sight is street vendors who provide food. These vendors often have wheelbarrow-like contraptions with a stove. When summoned, the vendor pulls his cart over and begins food preparation on the spot. Besides the more common rice, noodles, and soup, they also sell rujak, a mixed fruit salad that contains chili and peanuts.

Water is a precious commodity in Indonesia. This is particularly true

The fruit that looks like a weapon: the durian.

Indonesian street vendors can prepare virtually any type of food, from a full-course meal to a cup of coffee. These "starbikes" provide coffee at a fraction of the price of major brand names.

during the dry season, known as the kemarau. In general, water is not safe to drink from the tap, and must be boiled first to avoid getting sick. When water is provided in a restaurant, for example, it is offered warm to show that it has been boiled. Even ice should be avoided unless it is known to be from a safe source. Bottled water is a common alternative. Indonesians often have to drill wells or even borrow water from a neighbor rather than rely on water piped into their houses. The rainy season is supposed to bring fresh, clean water. However, it also causes floods in many places because the sewage and drainage systems are inadequate.

FYI FACT:

Rice is not only an important Indonesian food, but also serves as a symbol of life.

During the Sekaten Festival honoring the birth of the prophet Muhammad, Indonesian Muslims carry a food mound known as the gunungan. Getting a piece of the gunungan is supposed to bring good luck.

Celebrations and Commemorations

Everyone loves a celebration, and Indonesians are no exception. With so many different cultures, Indonesia has a large variety of festivals that appeal both to visitors and to residents.

Ramadan and the festival that ends it, called Lebaran, are two of the most important celebratory events for Muslims in Indonesia.

Each day during the month of Ramadan, Muslims over the age of 10 rise before sunrise and have a meal. During daylight hours, they fast—which means they don't eat or drink anything. The fast tests their spiritual values and self-discipline.

Lebaran celebrates the end of Ramadan and the resumption of normal patterns of eating and drinking. People wear new clothes, light firecrackers, prepare elaborate dinners at their homes, and visit friends and family. Often packets of woven coconut fronds with steamed rice inside are hung all over, like Christmas holly. During Lebaran the young ask forgiveness of the old, and the old do the same of the young.

Seventy days after Lebaran, the Idul Adha festival commemorates the Prophet Abraham's willingness to sacrifice his son as a sign of his devotion to Allah (the Muslim name for God). A ram was ultimately substituted for the boy. In modern Indonesia, a sheep or goat is often sacrificed. The appearance of these animals at markets means that Idul Adha is drawing near.

A fourth important Muslim observance is Sekaten, a week-long ceremony to mark the birth of the Prophet Muhammad. A few days before Sekaten begins, ceremonial food mounds called gunungan

FYI FACT:

Indonesians love to play badminton.

(GOO-noong-ahn) are prepared at the royal palace. During Sekaten itself the mounds are blessed and distributed to those who are waiting. Obtaining a piece of the gunungan is supposed to bring good harvests and good fortune.

Bali, which is primarily Hindu, has an important festival called Nyepi (NEE-ah-pee). It celebrates the New Year, and falls in March or April. Observed for the full 24 hours, it is a day of complete and total silence. There is no lighting of fires or traveling, lights must be kept low, and many people do not talk or eat. Volume from television and radio is kept very low. Tourists cannot use the beaches or go out onto the streets.

Galungan is a 10-day Hindu festival that celebrates the victory of good over evil. It is believed that during this time the gods and deceased relatives return to earth. Decorations and food are prepared as offerings. Galungan is based on the 210-day Balinese calendar, so the festival sometimes happens twice a year.

Buddhists celebrate Waisak, which honors the birth, death, and enlightenment of Buddha. Thousands of people gather at Borobudur, the ancient Buddhist temple in central Java. At two in the morning hundreds of monks and others carrying candles climb to the top of the temple. When the moon is at its fullest, they light

The Leberan feast celebrates the end of the fasting that takes place during the Muslim month of Ramadan, and many traditional Indonesian dishes are prepared.

Buddhist monks near the Sewu temple in Yogyakarta, Java, perform ceremonies during the Waisak holiday, which celebrates the birth, enlightenment, and death of Buddha.

more candles, meditate, and recite sacred verses. The festival usually occurs in May.

No matter what their religion, Indonesians celebrate Independence Day on August 17. Red and white banners and lighting displays appear throughout the country. So does the phrase "Dirgahayu RI," which means "Long Live the Republic of Indonesia." One highlight is an elaborate flag-raising ceremony. A huge parade in Jakarta on the following Sunday that draws countless numbers of participants and spectators is another.

These are some of the major festivals and celebrations in Indonesia. Given the large amount of different ethnic groups that live in Indonesia, there are many regional celebrations and festivals. Likewise, Indonesian weddings have many different customs and traditions. All are celebratory affairs that include as many people as possible. In fact, sometimes people get invited to several weddings in a single day!

A bride prays during her wedding on the island of Bali. Wedding receptions are very popular social events in Indonesia, and guests may attend several in one day.

Weddings are usually divided into the ceremony itself and the reception. Many people attend only the reception. Even if you receive an invitation, it is customary to ask permission first if you want to attend the actual ceremony as well.

Unlike American weddings, there is no dancing or alcohol at Indonesian weddings. It is considered rude to show up at a wedding after drinking somewhere else. The food served can be extensive. Many people just show up to have something to eat and pay their respects to the happy couple, particularly if they have another wedding to attend.

Although death certainly isn't a reason to celebrate, Indonesian customs for death also illustrate the nation's ethnic diversity.

Because Indonesia is a largely Muslim country, it is customary to bury a person within 24 hours of his or her death. The body is prepared for burial by family members. The head always faces Mecca, the birthplace of Muhammad. Before the face is covered, family and friends view it one final time and say a silent prayer. Normally, expressions of public grief are not practiced. White is the traditional color of mourning for Muslims.

The Torajan people of South Selawesi have long been known for their elaborate, almost festive funerals. The Torajan believe that the dead person's spirit enters Puya, a place for the dead. In Puya the spirits must demonstrate their social position. A person with an elevated position in the community has a fancy funeral.

On Bali, the Trunyan put a dead body under a Taru Menyan tree near Lake Kintamani, the island's largest lake. The tree's fragrance eliminates any odors from the corpse as it slowly decomposes. When only a skeleton remains, the skull is placed on a nearby stone platform.

Javanese funerals consist of numerous activities, especially the preparation of special meals known as selamatan. The first special meal is held on the day of the funeral, followed by another one three days later. Further observances come on the seventh day after the funeral, the 40th day, the 100th day, the first and second anniversaries, with the grandest on the 1000th day. By then, the Javanese believe, the dead person has found peace.

Indonesia is a sprawling country. Many different peoples live under the single umbrella of Indonesia. However, the slogan "unity through diversity" has proven to be more than just words. It has proven to be a successful way of life. Hopefully that philosophy can continue to point the way forward for Indonesia's future.

FYI FACT:

Indonesians do not cry when a person dies because they believe it indicates a weak soul.

Rujak

Spicy Fruit Salad

Rujak is one of the readily available treats from street vendors, and young people often eat it when they come home from school. It takes only moments to prepare and its strong flavors provide a quick pick-me-up.

Ingredients:
1 medium-sized can of pineapple chunks
2 bananas, peeled and chopped
3 green apples, peeled and chopped
1 small cucumber, peeled and sliced

Dressing:
1 teaspoon chili powder
1 tablespoon soy sauce
½ cup dark brown sugar
2 tablespoons lemon or lime juice

Preparation:
Prepare the following recipe with adult supervision:
1. Place all fruits and vegetables into a bowl and mix thoroughly.
2. In a separate bowl, combine dressing ingredients.
3. Pour the dressing over the fruits and vegetables. Chill before serving.

Shadow Puppets Theater

You can make your own Indonesian shadow puppets and shadow puppet theater, then put on a show. Shadow puppet shows take place behind the curtain, not in front of it like other puppets. A light shines on the puppets so the audience can see their shadows.

Puppet Materials:
Piece of cardboard
Pencil
Tape
Scissors
Dowels or other type of small pieces of wood
  such as chopsticks or ice cream sticks
Paper punch
Paper fasteners

Theater Materials:
White sheet
Bright light

Instructions
1. Make the puppet by drawing a character on the cardboard.
2. Cut it out. To have the arms and legs move separately from the rest of the puppet, draw them and cut out apart from the rest of the puppet.
3. Decorate your puppet however you desire.
4. If the arms and legs are supposed to move, attach these to the puppet with paper fasteners.
5. Tape the dowel or piece of wood to the puppet's body and to each moving part.
6. Make the theater by hanging a white sheet across a doorway. Put the light behind the sheet and turn it on. Hold the puppet between the light and the sheet, keeping it as close to the sheet as possible. You're ready to put on your show!

TIMELINE

Dates BCE
2 million–

500,000	Human ancestors called Homo erectus, or Java man, live in the area.

Dates CE

425	Buddhism comes to Sumatra.
700	Trade routes with China and India are formed.
825	The Buddhist temple Borobudur is completed.
1200s–1300s	Buddhist and Hindu kingdoms reach the peak of their power.
1500	Islam becomes the main religion in Indonesia.
1513	Portugal builds a fort at the site of present-day Jakarta.
1595	Cornelis de Houtman leads the first Dutch expedition to Indonesia.
1602	The Dutch East India Company is founded as a trading company.
1603	The Dutch establish a permanent trading post in West Java.
1670	All of Indonesia comes under Dutch rule.
1799	The Dutch East India Company goes bankrupt; due to the Dutch presence, the Indonesian islands are known as the Dutch East Indies.
1824	The Anglo-Dutch Treaty of 1824 divides the region; the Dutch take virtually all of Indonesia while the British claim Malaya, Singapore, and retain an interest in North Borneo.
1825	Prince Diponegoro leads his forces in the Java War, which begins because of a Dutch decision to build a road across land containing the tombs of the prince's parents; when it ends five years later 200,000 Indonesians and 15,000 Europeans have been killed.
1873	The Dutch effort to claim Aceh, which up until now had remained independent, results in a war that lasts until 1914.
1908	The Budi Utomo, or "Beautiful Endeavor," is founded with the goal of achieving independence for Indonesia.
1942	Japan occupies Indonesia during World War II.
1945	Indonesian nationalists declare that the country is independent and free from Dutch rule as World War II ends and the Japanese depart.
1949	After four years of warfare, the Dutch acknowledge the independence of Indonesia.
1950	Indonesia is admitted to the United Nations.
1967	Suharto becomes president and begins three decades of absolute rule.

1975	Indonesia invades East Timor and war breaks out between the two sides.
1997	The Asian economic crisis has a severe effect on Indonesia, causing the value of its currency to drastically decline.
1998	Suharto resigns as president.
1999	The first completely free parliamentary elections since 1955 are held.
2002	East Timor becomes independent.
2004	The first direct presidential elections occur as Susilo Bambang Yudhoyono is victorious; a tsunami resulting from an undersea earthquake smashes into Indonesia.
2008	Former President Suharto dies.
2009	President Susilo Bambang Yudhoyono is re-elected.
2014	The third direct presidential election takes place on July 9.

CHAPTER NOTES

Chapter One: A Tsunami Leads to Peace
1. Indian Ocean Tsunami Disaster in Asia, 2004 – National University of Singapore, http://www.crisp.nus.edu.sg/tsunami/tsunami.html
2. BBC News: Asia-Pacific—At-a-glance, Countries Hit, http://news.bbc.co.uk/2/hi/4126019.stm

Chapter Two: Indonesia's Early History
1. Justine Vaisutis, *Indonesia* (Oakland, California: Lonely Planet Publications, 2007), p. 37.
2. Indonesia History—History of Indonesia, indo.com, http://www.indo.com/indonesia/history.html

Chapter Three: The Rocky Road to Independence
1. Justine Vaisutis, *Indonesia* (Oakland, California: Lonely Planet Publications, 2007), p. 51.

Chapter Five: An Island Tour
1. Eric Oey (editor), *Java: Garden of the East* (Lincolnwood, Illinois: Passport Books, 1991), p. 20.
2. Ibid.
3. Ibid. p. 25.
4. Eric Oey (editor), *Sumatra: Island of Adventure* (Lincolnwood, Illinois: Passport Books, 1996), p. 17.
5. Ibid. p. 25.
6. Joshua Eliot, *Indonesia Handbook* (Chicago: Passport Books, 1996), p. 612.

Books

Benoit, Peter. *The Krakatau Eruption*. New York: Children's Press, 2011.

Cassanos, Lynda Cohen. *Indonesia*. Broomall, Pennsylvania: Mason Crest Publishers, 2010.

Gouri, Mirpuri. *Indonesia*. Tarrytown, New York: Marshall Cavendish Benchmark, 2012.

Kalman, Bobbie. *Spotlight On Indonesia*. New York: Crabtree, 2010.

Reynolds, Jan. *Cycle of Rice, Cycle of Life*. New York: Lee & Low Books, 2009.

On the Internet

About Indonesia
   http://kids.embassyofindonesia.org/aboutIndonesiacover.htm
   http://kids.yahoo.com/reference/world-factbook/country/id--Indonesia

Around the World—Indonesia, Time for Kids
   http://www.timeforkids.com/destination/indonesia

Around the World—Indonesia Timeline, Time for Kids
   http://www.timeforkids.com/destination/indonesia/history-timeline

Indonesia, kids.net.au
   http://encyclopedia.kids.net.au/page/in/Indonesia

Geography for Kids—Indonesia, Ducksters.com
   http://www.ducksters.com/geography/country.php?country=Indonesia

Books

Chatterji, B.R. *History of Indonesia*. Meerut, India: Meenakshi Prakashan, 1967.

Eliot, Joshua. *Indonesia Handbook*. Chicago: Passport Books, 1996.

Frederick, William H. and Robert L. Worden (editors). *Indonesia: A Country Study*. Washington, D.C: Federal Research Division, Library of Congress, 1993.

Hellwig, Tineke and Eric Tagliacozza (editors). *The Indonesian Reader*. Durham, North Carolina: Duke University Press, 2009.

Oey, Eric (editor). *Java: Garden of the East*. Lincolnwood, Illinois: Passport Books, 1991.

Oey, Eric (editor). *Sumatra: Island of Adventure*. Lincolnwood, Illinois: Passport Books, 1996.

Ricklefs, M.C. *A History of Modern Indonesia*. Bloomington, Indiana: Indiana University Press, 1981.

Saunders, Graham. *Culture Smart! Indonesia*. London: Kuperard, 2007.

Vaisutis, Justine. *Indonesia*. Oakland, California: Lonely Planet Publications, 2007.

Vlekke, Bernard H. *The Story of the Dutch East Indies*. Cambridge, Massachusetts: Harvard University Press, 1945.

Winterton, Bradley. *The Insider's Guide to Bali*. Edison, New Jersey: Hunter Publishing, 1989.

Zainu'ddin, Ailsa. *A Short History of Indonesia*. New York: Praeger, 1970.

On the Internet

Reid, Wayne. "The Indonesian Language," Bali: The Online Travel Guide
http://home.mira.net/~wreid/bali_lng.html

Rustan, Mario. Funeral Customs
http://www.st.rim.or.jp/~cycle/MYfunerE.HTML

Indonesia—The CIA World Factbook
https://www.cia.gov/library/publications/the-world-factbook/geos/id.html

Indonesian Food: What Indonesians Eat
http://indonesia.elga.net.id/indoway/food.html

Sipiro-Piso Waterfall: Destinations in Indonesia.

Wonderful Indonesia, Indonesia's Official Tourism Website
http://www.indonesia.travel/en/destination/52/sipiso-piso-waterfall

Indonesia Holidays & Festivals. About.com Southeast Asia Travel
http://goseasia.about.com/od/eventsfestival1/tp/indonesia_fest.htm

Indonesian Wedding Ceremonies and Customs. Living in Indonesia
http://www.expat.or.id/info/weddings.html

Indonesia Timeline
http://www.worldatlas.com/webimage/countrys/asia/indonesia/idtimeln.htm

GLOSSARY

archipelago (ahr-kuh-PEHL-uh-go)—A large group or chain of islands.

consolidate (kuhn-SAHL-uh-dayt)—To bring together.

cultivate (KUHL-tih-veyt)—To prepare and work land in order to raise crops.

dissension (dih-SEHN-shun)—Strong disagreement.

endemic (ehn-DEHM-ik)—Prevalent in or restricted to a particular geographic location.

exotic (egg-ZAH-tik)—Unusual or strange.

exterminate (ek-STUHR-muh-nayt)—Totally destroy.

harass (huh-RASS)—Bother repeatedly.

mammoth (MAM-uhth)—Huge, immense.

momentous (moh-MEHN-tuhss)—Having great importance or significance.

motto (MAHT-oh)—A word, phrase, sentence, etc., that expresses the purpose or spirit of a person or organization.

nutrient (NOO-tree-uhnt)—A form of nourishment.

oust (OUST)—To remove.

parasite (PAIR-uh-sight)—An organism that lives in or on another organism of a different species and obtains nourishment from that source.

percussive (per-KUH-sihv)—Relating to percussion, the striking of materials with sticks, hammers, or hands to get musical tones.

populous (POP-yoo-luhss)—Having a large population.

ravage (RAV-ij)—Do devastating damage.

repressive (ree-PRESS-ihv)—Holding down, stifling.

surged (SURJD)—Rushed forward.

staple (STAY-puhl)—A basic food.

turmoil (TUHR-moil)—Great commotion or confusion.

INDEX

Aceh   9, 10, 11, 16, 18
Acenese   39
Affandi   31
All Indonesian Youth Congress   19
Badui   40
Bali   18, 24, 27, 33, 37, 40
Balinese   40
Batak   39
Batavia   21
Borneo   18, 36
Borobudur   15, 52
Budi Utomo   19
Bugis   40
Chinese   42
cultivation system   19
Darwin, Charles   35
Darul Islam   22
Dayaks   36, 41
death observances   54
durian   47
Dutch East India Company   16
East Timor   23, 24
Free Aceh Movement   11
Galungan   52
Habibie, B.J.   24
House of Regional Representatives
   27
Idul Adha   51
Jakarta   21, 24, 27, 35
Java   18, 19, 27, 33, 34
Javanese   40
Kalimantan   33, 34, 36, 41
Kartini, Raden Adjeng   30
Krakatau   9, 34
Lake Kintamuni   55
Lake Toba   37, 39
Leberan   51
Mada, Gajah   17, 29
Malays   15
Majapahit   16, 29

Mataram   15
Minahasa   41
Minangkabau   39
Mt. Semeru   33
National University of Singapore   10
Nyepi   52
Obama, Barack   26
Partai Komunis Indonesia   19
Partai Nasional Indonesia   19, 30
People's Consultative Assembly   27
Polo, Marco   16
rafflesia   34
Ramadan   51
rambutan   47
Samosir   37
Sarekat Islam   19
Seketen   51
Soedirohoesodo, Wahidin   19
Sriwijaya   15
Sundanese   40
Suharto   23, 24, 29
Sukarno   19, 21, 22, 23, 29, 30
Sukarnoputri, Megawati   31
Sulawesi   33, 35, 36, 40
Sumatra   9, 10, 16, 18, 33, 34, 39
Timor   23, 33
Toraja   40
Torajan   55
Tribhuwana, Queen   29
Trunyan   55
Vereenigde Oost-Indische Compagnie
   16, 17, 18
Waisak   52
Wallace, Alfred Russel   35
wayang kulit   40
weddings   53
West Sumatra   19
Wuruk, Hiram   16, 29
Yudhoyono, Susilo Bambang   27

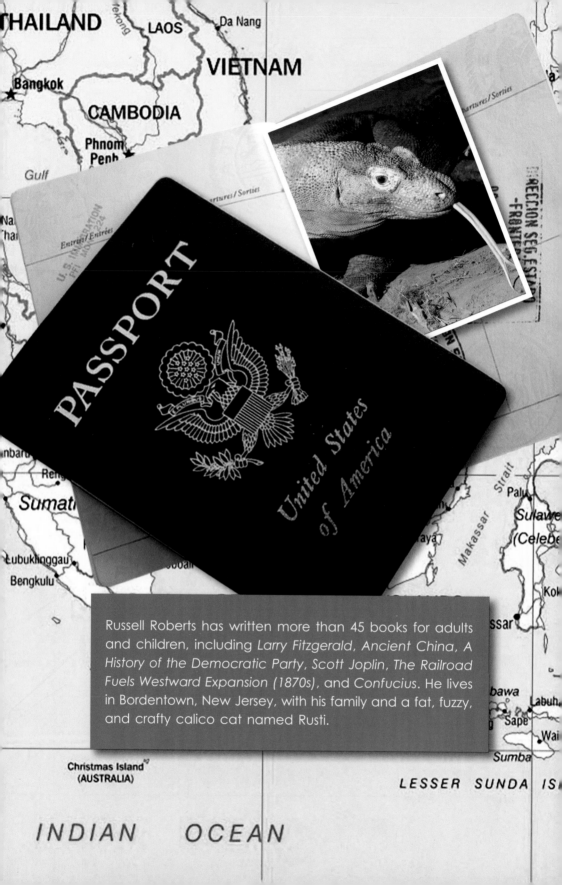

Russell Roberts has written more than 45 books for adults and children, including *Larry Fitzgerald*, *Ancient China*, *A History of the Democratic Party*, *Scott Joplin*, *The Railroad Fuels Westward Expansion (1870s)*, and *Confucius*. He lives in Bordentown, New Jersey, with his family and a fat, fuzzy, and crafty calico cat named Rusti.